VIRT1

MW00776700

HOSPITALITY
Welcoming the Stranger

Catherine Upchurch

Little Rock
Scripture Study

*A ministry of the Diocese of Little Rock
in partnership with Liturgical Press*

Nihil obstat: Jerome Kodell, OSB, *Censor Librorum.*
Imprimatur: ✢ Anthony B. Taylor, Bishop of Little Rock, February 3, 2017.

Cover design by Ann Blattner. Cover photo: Thinkstock Images by Getty. Used with permission.

Photos/illustrations: Page 6, Lightstock. Used with permission. Pages 10 (*Jacob greeting Joseph*) and 17 (*Loaves and the Fishes*), Wikimedia Commons. Used with permission. Pages 12, 13, 14, 21, 23, 25 (both), 29, 34, 36, Thinkstock Images by Getty. Used with permission. Page 17, Wikimedia Commons. Used with permission. Page 40, maps from *Little Rock Catholic Study Bible*, created by Robert Cronan of Lucidity Information Design, LLC © 2011 Little Rock Scripture Study. Used with permission.

ISBN: 978-0-8146-4573-4 (print); 978-0-8146-4599-4 (ebook)

Contents

Introduction

Alive in the Word brings you resources to deepen your understanding of Scripture, offer meaning for your life today, and help you to pray and act in response to God's word.

Use any volume of **Alive in the Word** in the way best suited to you.

- **For individual learning and reflection,** consider this an invitation to prayerfully journal in response to the questions you find along the way. And be prepared to move from head to heart and then to action.
- **For group learning and reflection,** arrange for three sessions where you will use the material provided as the basis for faith sharing and prayer. You may ask group members to read each chapter in advance and come prepared with questions answered. In this kind of session, plan to be together for about an hour. Or, if your group prefers, read and respond to the questions together without advance preparation. With this approach, it's helpful to plan on spending more time for each group session in order to adequately work through each chapter.

- **For a parish-wide event or use within a larger group,** provide each person with a copy of this volume, and allow time during the event for quiet reading, group discussion and prayer, and then a final commitment by each person to some simple action in response to what he or she learned.

This volume explores the theme of hospitality as one of the **Virtues for Disciples.** Each of us is called to be a disciple, a follower of Christ. The life of a disciple is challenging but it is the most fulfilling way to live. Called by name by the God who created us, we are shaped by the teachings of Christ and continually guided by the Holy Spirit. As we grow more deeply into this identity as disciples of Jesus Christ, we discover the valuable virtues that mark God's people.

Duty to Strangers

Begin by asking God to assist you in your prayer and study. Then read through the three passages from the Old Testament to consider God's law regarding duty to strangers.

Exodus 22:20
[20]You shall not oppress or afflict a resident alien, for you were once aliens residing in the land of Egypt.

Leviticus 19:33-34
[33]When an alien resides with you in your land, do not mistreat such a one. [34]You shall treat the alien who resides with you no differently than the natives born among you; you shall love the alien as yourself; for you too were once aliens in the land of Egypt. I, the LORD, am your God.

Leviticus 23:22
[22]When you reap the harvest of your land, you shall not be so thorough that you reap the field to its very edge, nor shall you gather the gleanings of your harvest. These things you shall leave for the poor and the alien. I, the LORD, am your God.

Setting the Scene

Biblical hospitality is more than setting a lovely table or welcoming a guest with warmth and generosity. It is a reflection of God's own nature and God's own actions of welcoming love recounted in numerous ways throughout the Bible. In the past as well as the present, God interacts with people in the particular locations and cultures where we live and sets patterns for how we are to live in response to God's hospitality.

The ancient Near East was the general location of God's people from Old Testament times through Jesus' day and into the earliest generation of Christian communities. Specifically, the area was known variously as Canaan (named for those who occupied the land prior to the arrival of the Hebrews), Israel and Judah (names for the tribal areas after Hebrew settlement), Palestine (a Greek name for the land of the Philistines), and more generally the Holy Land. (See the map on page 40.)

Inhabitants of this land were and are subject to the climate and geographical challenges that come with living in such a vast and largely arid place. As was typical in such dry places, the people were often nomadic, traveling to find favorable conditions for their cattle, their families, and, if they were fortunate, some meager crops. In antiquity, many people dwelled in simple huts or tents and usually lived together with extended family or clans.

When travel was necessary—for simple trade or attending religious festivals or moving one's family to escape famine or war—it would have been essential to depend on the kindness of strangers. An inn, such as we hear about in the parable of the Good Samaritan (Luke 10:25-37), would have been rare. Simple kindnesses such as providing water for travelers or a loaf of bread were common. And providing humble dwelling in one's home or on one's land would have been common as well. Such acts of hospitality were necessary for survival.

> What can you recall from a time when you relied on the hospitality of others or when you were called upon to host a relative stranger?

For God's people, the Ten Commandments given to Moses formed the framework of their cultural and religious experience. These basic tenets made it clear that their lives were to be governed by love of God (the first three commands) and love of neighbor (the final seven). They understood that all of life's interactions should reflect the divine instructions given at Sinai. And so, as they traveled together and then settled in the land of Canaan, their laws expanded to reflect this sensitivity to God's will in every aspect of life.

Love God, love neighbor

If we were to count all the laws now found in the Pentateuch (the first five books of the Bible), we would find over 600 statutes that came to constitute the Law of Moses. Among these laws we find numerous references to treating others in a way that reflects a covenant understanding of God. Specifically, there are many laws about the just treatment of resident aliens—that is, those who are not full members of an Israelite clan or family but who reside with and among them. We will look at three such laws, one from Exodus and two from Leviticus.

> *Each of the three passages will be considered separately for a deeper understanding.*

Understanding the Scenes Themselves

Exodus 22:20
²⁰You shall not oppress or afflict a resident alien, for you were once aliens residing in the land of Egypt.

What is a "resident alien" in the context of the Bible? In modern times this language refers to a legal status related to formal immigration into a country. Formal and legal processes for immigration or migration in the ancient world, however, would not have existed.

Migrating from one land to another was common and accepted, and there are ample stories of such patterns in the Bible, particularly in the Old Testament. Consider just a few examples:

What experiences have you had of feeling like an outsider? (This could occur in a neighborhood or town, a parish or a workplace.)

- Abraham and Sarah and their relatives moved in response to God's call from Haran, in modern-day Turkey, to the land of Canaan, now Israel. They were aliens among the Canaanites but before long a famine swept through the land, and Abraham took his family to Egypt where they were once again aliens (see Gen 12:1-10).
- Jacob and his many family members migrated at a later time from Canaan back to Egypt in order to survive during a famine. Ironically, it was Jacob's younger son Joseph, earlier sold into slavery by his brothers, who rose to prominence in Egypt and could provide safety and land for his father and his brother's families (see Gen 42–47).
- Even the young David, following murderous threats of King Saul, fled to the land of Moab, an enemy territory, where he found safety for his parents as well (see 1 Sam 22:1-5).
- The book of Ruth tells the story of a family that migrated from Bethlehem at a time of famine into the land of Moab where the sons married Moabite women. Once the famine had lifted years later and the women were left widowed, Naomi returned to her native Bethlehem with one daughter-in-law who would then be the foreigner (see Ruth 1:1-22).

Perhaps the largest migration is recounted in the book of Exodus. The Hebrew slaves, oppressed and abused by the pharaoh of Egypt, were released from their captivity and wandered through the Sinai desert before arriving in the land of the Canaanites. God provided not only a passage to freedom for them, but established them in a land that allowed them to settle into communities, grow crops, and feed cattle. God acted as redeemer and host.

It is this foundational experience of having once been a minority population in a foreign land, having been slaves with few rights, and having been freed by God, that shaped a ragtag group of Hebrews into a people—and eventually into a nation. They experienced anything but hospitality in Egypt, and so their law enshrined that lesson by requiring a certain basic respect for the strangers in their midst.

> When has a previous experience of some kind served as a life lesson for you?

Leviticus 19:33-34

³³When an alien resides with you in your land, do not mistreat such a one. ³⁴You shall treat the alien who resides with you no differently than the natives born among you; you shall love the alien as yourself; for you too were once aliens in the land of Egypt. I, the LORD, am your God.

This passage from Leviticus parallels the passage from Exodus 22, with some added features that deserve attention.

The first word in verse 33, "when," indicates that foreigners, outsiders, aliens will live among God's people. The presence of foreigners was

not a remote possibility, something that may happen at some point in the future, but a reality of living at that time. Given that reality, God's people were told in verse 33 not to mistreat them.

"Do not mistreat" sets up parameters, a set of guidelines to prevent the kind of situations that Israel's ancestors found themselves in when in Egypt. One could argue whether certain actions were in fact mistreatment. But "treat them no differently than the natives born among you" (v. 34) indicates there are no parameters. There are no limits or conditions. Treating others like family requires love.

We hear a familiar ring to "love the alien as yourself" in the New Testament. When Jesus is asked to identify the greatest commandment (Matt 22:34-40), he responds by saying "love the Lord, your God, with all your heart, with all your soul, and with all your mind." And then he equates this with a second command to "love your neighbor as yourself." In Luke's version, the scholar of the law, hoping to identify his neighbor, questions Jesus further. Jesus replies with the now well-known parable of the Good Samaritan (Luke 10:29-37). The neighbor is the one in need *and* the neighbor is the foreigner who offers compassionate help, who provided the necessary means for the man who had been robbed to re-

> How would you describe the difference between banning mistreatment and requiring love? Does it challenge you in any way to know that God's law requires such love?

> Who is our "neighbor" today? Who are we being asked to love in practical ways?

cover. Through his care and financial assistance, the Samaritan offered a much-needed hospitality.

Leviticus 23:22

[22]When you reap the harvest of your land, you shall not be so thorough that you reap the field to its very edge, nor shall you gather the gleanings of your harvest. These things you shall leave for the poor and the alien. I, the LORD, am your God.

Leviticus 23 outlines the provisions that must be made available to those who are in need. Gleaning was a way of providing food for those on the margins of society—those who were orphaned and widowed, those who were aliens living among the population. It was a sacred obligation to assure that food was on the table.

In our world today, especially in developed countries where massive machinery does most of the harvesting, it is hard to imagine what might be left on a grapevine or a stalk of wheat or barley, or how fruit could still be available after the trees have been so thoroughly shaken in the grips of steel machinery. In the ancient world, and even throughout much of the developing world today, harvesting consisted of manual labor, and it took weeks for workers to make their way through fields and orchards, picking crops as they ripened and then going back through as

more became ready to harvest. It was after the first harvest that those in need were allowed to "glean" what was still on the vine or the stock or the tree.

Many of us are not in the business of farming. Nonetheless, how could we cultivate an attitude of sharing from the best we have to offer?

The most famous biblical illustration of gleaning is found in the book of Ruth. Naomi, widowed in Moab, returns home to her native Bethlehem with her Moabite daughter-in-law, Ruth. With no male family members still living, Naomi has to rely on the hospitality of extended family or landowners. Ruth, also without male family members—and an alien in Bethlehem—must rely on Naomi and her connections in order for the two women to survive. A distant relative, a landowner by the name of Boaz, allowed the younger Ruth to glean the fields (see Ruth 2), and he went out of his way to assure that her harvest was ample for the two women and that she was safe among his workers.

Boaz offered Ruth, an alien, the hospitality guaranteed by God's law, and eventually he married her and produced an heir who would be the grandfather of King David (Ruth 4:13-22).

Praying the Word / Sacred Reading

Allow the words of the three passages of Scripture above to lead you into prayer. What responses to God's Word do you want to make? How do you feel challenged, threatened, affirmed, or energized? Bring these responses to God and listen for God to speak to your heart.

You may want to pray with the words of this prayer:

O God, liberator of those oppressed and forgotten,
    help us to see in those who are outsiders among us
    the opportunity to offer the sustenance of food and shelter
    and the gift of familial love.

O God, revealer of truth,
    pull back whatever blinders prevent us from seeing our own "strangeness,"
    our own need and lack of belonging,
    so that we can open ourselves
    to your welcome and loving embrace.

O God, breaker of barriers,
    be with us as we reach across the differences that could divide us,
    so that our commitment is unity,
    our preference is hospitality,
    and our desire is to love as you love, to welcome as you welcome.

Living the Word

Investigate national or local organizations that help to provide food, housing, and skills training to those who are in need of assistance. You may want to search the Internet using keywords such as gleaning, housing, and practical hospitality. These organizations in some ways embody the hospitality of God and the hospitality that we are called to exhibit in our lives as Christians. How might you become involved?

The Feeding of the Five Thousand

Begin by asking God to assist you in your prayer and study. Then read through the account sometimes known as the multiplication of loaves and fish as described in Mark 6:34-44.

Mark 6:34-44

34When [Jesus] disembarked and saw the vast crowd, his heart was moved with pity for them, for they were like sheep without a shepherd; and he began to teach them many things. 35By now it was already late and his disciples approached him and said, "This is a deserted place and it is already very late. 36Dismiss them so that they can go to the surrounding farms and villages and buy themselves something to eat." 37He said to them in reply, "Give them some food yourselves." But they said to him, "Are we to buy two hundred days' wages worth of food and give it to them to eat?" 38He asked them, "How many loaves do you have? Go and see." And when they had found out they said, "Five loaves and two fish." 39So he gave orders to have them sit down in groups on the green grass. 40The people took their places in rows by hundreds and by fifties. 41Then, taking the five loaves and the two fish and looking up to heaven, he said the blessing, broke the loaves, and gave them to [his] disciples to set before the people; he also divided the two fish among them all. ⁴²They all ate and were satisfied. ⁴³And they picked up twelve wicker baskets full of fragments and what was left of the fish. ⁴⁴Those who ate [of the loaves] were five thousand men.

Following a few minutes of quiet reflection on the passage above, consider the information provided in "Setting the Scene."

Setting the Scene

The ministry of Jesus took place on a rather small stage in human terms. Israel was a nation that occupied a sliver of land on the eastern shore of the Mediterranean Sea. With the exception of the area right near the Jordan River that ran through the spine of the country, and the area around the Sea of Galilee, it was a largely arid landscape (see map on page 40). Little wonder, then, that the areas with concentrated populations were more fertile regions with access to fresh water and the ability to sustain crops.

In the scene described in Mark 6, Jesus and his followers are in the populated region around Galilee and have gone off in a boat by themselves to what they hope will be a deserted place. The presumption is that they launched out onto the Sea of Galilee (also known as Lake Chennereth, or later, the Sea of Tiberius) heading toward a "deserted place."

In Mark's version of events Jesus' closest followers had already witnessed Jesus teaching in parables and healing those around him, stirring up controversy among the scribes and Pharisees. Jesus had already calmed the storm on the sea and had been rejected in Nazareth. Just prior to the loaves and fishes scene in Mark, the disciples would have heard of the execution of John the Baptist. They are surely weary, excited, and frightened all at the same time when Jesus takes them away to "rest a while" (Mark 6:31).

But there is no rest for the weary, at least not in the way we might welcome if we were in the shoes of Jesus' disciples. They are met by a "vast crowd" on the shore, a crowd with hungers that must be fed—hungers both spiritual and physical. Jesus becomes the hospitable host to those whose hungers draw them away from their homes and routines to be with him, watching and listening.

The account of Jesus feeding a multitude of people is found six times in the four gospels; it is the only miracle that is consistently reported in all four gospels. The feeding of 5000 can be found here in Mark 6:31-44, as well as in Matthew 14:13-21, Luke 9:10-17, and John 6:5-15. The feeding of an additional 4000 is found later in Mark 8:1-10 and in Matthew 15:32–16:10. Such a repeated emphasis communicates how important it was that Jesus attended to the hungers of those whom he found along the way.

In your experience, when you feel the need to be "recharged," how have you reacted when your plans are interrupted?

We will consider the above passage from Mark a few verses at a time, taking time to respond to the questions found in the margins.

Understanding the Scene Itself

[34]When [Jesus] disembarked and saw the vast crowd, his heart was moved with pity for them, for they were like sheep without a shepherd; and he began to teach them many things.

We might picture the scene: a boat full of weary men arrives in a place they hope to find restful only to discover that the crowds made it to the opposite shore ahead of them. The verbs tell us much about how Jesus responded to those on the shore. He saw, he was moved with pity, and he taught. Jesus focused on *their* need and responded with a course of action. He welcomed them rather than sending them away. He recognized in them a hunger that could only be satisfied with what he could share about God and the kingdom of God.

If Jesus were to meet you right now, what "hunger" might he see in you?

Jesus' "heart was moved with pity." In our use of the word today, when we pity someone we feel sorrow or anguish for them; we might even feel a certain relief that their experience is not our own. Far from a simple emotional sadness or feeling of concern, the word translated here as "pity" could also be translated as compassion or merciful love. Compassion and mercy move us beyond feeling to doing, beyond emotion to action. We might pity someone from a distance, or we might pity them and wish there was something we could do, but the pity spoken of here in the Bible requires a response and action on behalf of others in need.

The reason Jesus is moved on their behalf is because they are "like sheep without a shepherd." In Israel's tradition, religious and political leaders were often compared with shepherds, most often as a way to critique those who did not give the attention needed to their people, their flock. Some samples may be helpful:

Compassion and mercy move us beyond emotion to action.

- Moses prayed that God would set over the community "someone who will be their leader in battle and who will lead them out and bring them in, that the LORD's community may not be like sheep without a shepherd" (Num 27:17).
- Centuries later, Jeremiah is critical but also offers hope when he speaks God's message: "Woe to the shepherds who destroy and scatter the flock of the Lord. . . . I myself will gather the remnant of my flock from all the lands to which I have banished them and bring them back to their folds" (Jer 23:1, 3).
- Similarly, Ezekiel, reflecting the period of Babylonian exile, condemns the leaders of Israel whose neglect led to the downfall of their nation. "Woe to shepherds of Israel

who have been pasturing themselves! Should not the shepherds pasture the flock? . . . You did not strengthen the weak nor heal the sick nor bind up the injured. You did not bring back the stray or seek the lost but ruled them harshly and brutally. So they were scattered for lack of a shepherd" (Ezek 34:2, 4-5).

What does this metaphor or image of Jesus as the Good Shepherd reveal about the kind of leadership he values?

One of the key ways that we have come to know Jesus in the New Testament is connected to the image of the Good Shepherd (John 10:11-15; Heb 13:20-21; 1 Pet 2:24-25; Rev 7:17). In contrast to those religious and political leaders who lost their sheep or led them astray, Jesus becomes for them (and for us) the Good Shepherd who knows his sheep and knows what they need. In this scene from Mark, the crowd needs God's wisdom—and so Jesus teaches them.

[35]By now it was already late and his disciples approached him and said, "This is a deserted place and it is already very late. [36]Dismiss them so that they can go to the surrounding farms and villages and buy themselves something to eat." [37]He said to them in reply, "Give them some food yourselves." But they said to him, "Are we to buy two hundred days' wages worth of food and give it to them to eat?"

Remember, these disciples and Jesus had come to this place already weary. After the teaching, the disciples are ready to move folks along, perhaps to return to their original plans for peace and quiet and to have something to eat for themselves (see Mark 6:30-33). Their words sound a note of concern for those who are gathered, but the response of Jesus tells us that their concern should be about meeting the needs of the crowd rather than sending them away.

Jesus challenges his disciples to feed the people themselves. He modeled how to do this when he saw the crowd's need for wisdom and leadership and stopped to teach them. He provided nourishment for their souls. Now their need is physical nourishment, and the disciples are charged to meet that need. Both forms of nourishment can be seen as forms of hospitality—setting a banquet with the food of sound teaching and the food that will nourish their bodies.

Naturally, the disciples' first thought is "how?" What can they do to provide for so many? And how will they do it in a place that is "desolate," isolated? They are being logical, for certain, but Jesus is asking them to be attentive to need, to trust in God's provision, and to act before they give in to defeat.

Perhaps Jesus is preparing them for the time when he will not be physically present, when they (and we) will be the hands, feet, heart, eyes, and ears of Jesus. He has been a shepherd who knows his sheep, and he is preparing them to be

In what areas of your life are you being invited to trust God more fully?

shepherds also. He has hosted the crowd and fed them with God's Word, and he is asking them to be hosts and provide food for their journeys home.

How might you respond to Jesus' command to address the hungers of our world? Where do you begin?

[38] He asked them, "How many loaves do you have? Go and see." And when they had found out they said, "Five loaves and two fish." [39] So he gave orders to have them sit down in groups on the green grass. [40] The people took their places in rows by hundreds and by fifties.

Rather than give in to the panic the disciples displayed, and rather than focusing on what they did not have, Jesus asked them to take stock of what they *did* have. What could they put to use for the needs of the people? What could they offer that was already there among them?

In some ways this is a basic question of hospitality—what is already here that I can offer you? Jesus, like any good host, knows that the priorities are to create an environment of welcome and to meet the needs of those perceived as guests (even those "guests" who come unannounced as this crowd did by the shore).

Hospitality is not only about providing food. What are the treasures you have access to that could be multiplied to meet peoples' needs?

Mark describes the scene in such an orderly way: the grass is green and welcoming, and the people are seated in rows. This latter detail might be a way of recalling the account in Exodus 18:21 of Moses being instructed by his father-in-law to find a way to meet the needs of the people by assigning others to take responsibility over groups of "hundreds, of fifties, and of tens."

⁴¹Then, taking the five loaves and the two fish and looking up to heaven, he said the blessing, broke the loaves, and gave them to [his] disciples to set before the people; he also divided the two fish among them all. ⁴²They all ate and were satisfied. ⁴³And they picked up twelve wicker baskets full of fragments and what was left of the fish. ⁴⁴Those who ate [of the loaves] were five thousand men.

God fed those wandering in the desert on their way to the Promised Land with manna and quail (Exod 16:4-15; Deut 8:3). Jesus, centuries later, is in the midst of people who are hungry for God's promises and for food. He feeds those at the lakeshore with loaves and fish. It would not have been lost on them that the hospitality of God learned in the desert by their ancestors was now being shared again through the action of Jesus and his followers.

In ancient times, to give a blessing was to bless a person. In this case, Jesus blesses God who has provided the food that will be multiplied and shared. God has set aside this food especially for their use. It was in their midst all along, and it took an act of faith for that food to be recognized as the divine gift that it was and how it would provide for their needs.

To take, bless, break, and give are the actions we associate with the Last Supper and with our celebrations of the Eucharist in our parishes. (See Matt 26:26-28; Mark 14:22-24; Luke 22:14-20.) The feeding of the multitude is told in a way intended to prefigure this most distinct gift of God's own Son, the gift of his body and blood at the Last Supper. These actions—taking, blessing, breaking, and giving—have become the most profound actions of sacred hospitality. God sets a feast for us that welcomes us into the kingdom that will outlast all others, the kingdom of God.

Those on the shores of the Sea of Galilee that day "ate and were satisfied," and even had leftovers that could be shared with others. The hospitality of God, expressed so beautifully in this scene with Jesus, his disciples, and a vast crowd of followers, is a continuous gift. It begins with what is already in our midst, whether it is actual food or other more intangible gifts such as care and concern, joy and wisdom. Those gifts, given to us first by God and then returned to God, will be multiplied so that all are welcomed and satisfied.

The next time you participate in your parish Mass, take note of the various ways we are invited to experience God's hospitality.

Praying the Word / Sacred Reading

There are so many ways to pray with a scene described so fully in the Bible. One way is to place yourself in the scene and imagine the details and the responses of those around you. Speak to God about what you see and feel.

- You might imagine yourself as one of the followers who got in the boat with Jesus hoping for some rest and time to recharge. What do you feel when you reach the shore, and instead of quiet you encounter the humming of the crowd? How would you feel later when Jesus tells you to feed them? What do you experience as the meager amount of food meets the needs of the people?
- You might instead be one of those who made their way around the shoreline to hear more from Jesus. What hopes do you bring with you? What are your expectations when you've made an effort to be in his presence? How has Jesus surpassed your expectations?

Living the Word

Consider the following:

- *Make an effort to pay close attention to the people around you. What do they appear to be hungry for? What draws them together and what concerns them? As a follower of Jesus, what gifts already in your midst might you share with these same people? Could you invite someone to come to church or to Bible study as a way of helping address their hungers?*

- *On the other hand, take some time to consider ways that the followers of Jesus have provided the nourishment you need. Who reached out to you when you were hungry for security, wisdom, or assistance? Go out of your way to say thanks in person or in a note of gratitude. Help build the kingdom by acknowledging how you have been fed.*

The Exercise of Hospitality

> Ask God's direction and understanding as you prayerfully read three brief passages from the New Testament.

Romans 12:9-13
⁹Let love be sincere; hate what is evil, hold on to what is good; ¹⁰love one another with mutual affection; anticipate one another in showing honor. ¹¹Do not grow slack in zeal, be fervent in spirit, serve the Lord. ¹²Rejoice in hope, endure in affliction, persevere in prayer. ¹³Contribute to the needs of the holy ones, exercise hospitality.

1 Peter 4:7-10

[7]The end of all things is at hand. Therefore, be serious and sober for prayers. [8]Above all, let your love for one another be intense, because love covers a multitude of sins. [9]Be hospitable to one another without complaining. [10]As each one has received a gift, use it to serve one another as good stewards of God's varied grace.

Hebrews 13:1-2

[1]Let mutual love continue. [2]Do not neglect hospitality, for through it some have unknowingly entertained angels.

Consider some important background information as you begin to ponder the above passages.

Setting the Scene

In the New Testament, originally written primarily in Greek, the word used for hospitality is *philoxenia*. It combines two concepts: *phileo*, which means the love that is between friends and among family; and *xenos*, denoting outsiders or strangers. *Xenos* has even been used to describe those perceived to be enemies. Basically, hospitality is love of the stranger, the outsider.

Philoxenia certainly involves the things we connect with hospitality in contemporary society—things like providing a warm welcome, hearty meals, even beauty and comfort, but linking these things with an outsider or an enemy causes us to pause and wonder. It might even cause us some discomfort. But this quality or virtue is a necessary part of being a Christian. Some may exercise hospitality more easily than others because of their temperament or talents, but *all* are called to exercise hospitality as an expression of our relationship with Christ.

The selected passages from Paul's letter to the Romans, the first of Peter's letters, and the sermon we know as the book of Hebrews tell us that hospitality was at the heart of the early church. As these early Christian communities were being shaped, their leaders promoted the lessons taught by Jesus in his words and his deeds. Hospitality was part and parcel of his life as he traveled from place to place accepting hospitality from strangers, even some who plotted to destroy him (e.g., Mark 2:29-31; Luke 5:27-32; Luke 7:36-39; 10:38-42), providing lessons about hospitality (e.g., Matt 5:46-48; 7:12; Luke 19:1-10), and sending his disciples to do the same (e.g., Mark 6:7-10). Hospitality was also one of the conditions listed for those who would enter the kingdom of heaven (Matt 25:35-36).

> Why do you think hospitality may not receive the level of attention given to other Christian virtues?

As you explore the meaning of each of the passages, continue to pause to respond to the questions in a group discussion or in your own reflection.

Understanding the Scenes Themselves

Romans 12:9-13

[9]Let love be sincere; hate what is evil, hold on to what is good; [10]love one another with mutual affection; anticipate one another in showing honor. [11]Do not grow slack in zeal, be fervent in spirit, serve the Lord. [12]Rejoice in hope, endure in affliction, persevere in prayer. [13]Contribute to the needs of the holy ones, exercise hospitality.

Paul's letter to the Romans is arguably one of his most developed and persuasive. He invites believers to live in the freedom of the grace poured out in Christ and spells out the implications for living in community. The twelfth chapter of Romans contains one message—unity—in two sections. The first (vv. 3-8) employs the metaphor of the body, appealing for unity by describing the importance of all parts, and the second section (vv. 9-21) offers instructions for living healthily in community.

It is in this second section that we find our reference to hospitality. Verse 9, "Let love be sincere," could also be translated as "love is not hypocritical" or "love must be genuine." The remaining verses offer examples of this type of love from the day-to-day give-and-take of living with others and forming true community. Basically there are six couplets or pairings that might be paraphrased as follows:

- Hate evil, and cling to what is good (v. 9)
- Show mutual affection, and seek opportunities to honor each other (v. 10)
- Don't be complacent, but be fervent (v. 11)
- Serve God, and rejoice in hope (v. 11b, 12)
- Endure hardship, and be steadfast in prayer (v. 12)
- Be generous in meeting needs, and offer hospitality (v. 13)

Because of the freely given grace that Paul speaks of throughout Romans, those who are followers of Christ are expected to live in such a way that their love is evident. One important manifestation of that love is hospitality.

1 Peter 4:7-10
[7]**The end of all things is at hand. Therefore, be serious and sober for prayers. [8]Above all, let your love for one another be intense, because love covers a multitude of sins. [9]Be hospitable to one another without complaining. [10]As each one has received a gift, use it to serve one another as good stewards of God's varied grace.**

Baptism is the center point of the First Letter of Peter. It is baptism that communicates one's dignity and calling; it is baptism that shapes one's actions in the world; and it is baptism that strengthens those who are persecuted and suffering. We might look on this letter as an extended lesson on the impact of baptism in the daily struggle of living.

Which of these instructions or directives might need more attention in your faith community?

How might we foster hospitality as a vital aspect of Christian discipleship?

This letter was written at a time when being a Christian could be costly. The Roman Empire had sanctioned the persecution and execution of Christians, which were carried out with varying degrees of intensity for about 250 years. That highly charged atmosphere led people to contemplate the end times and led Christian leaders to urge the church to cling to those attributes and virtues that distinguished them as true followers of Christ.

The priority of love ("above all") is not unique here. It dominates Paul's writings as well, and it may be especially clear when Paul extols the excellence of love in 1 Corinthians 13, ending with these words: "So faith, hope, love remain, these three; but the greatest of these is love."

In 1 Peter, love should be intense or constant because "love covers a multitude of sins" (4:8). The full meaning of this saying has been explored by scholars and preachers for centuries. "Covering" sins is definitely not hiding them, but more probably it means forgiving or overlooking them. We might wonder, then, does such love cover the sins of the one who embodies love, or the sins of the one who needs forgiveness, or maybe all involved?

> So faith, hope, love remain, these three; but the greatest of these is love.
>
> 1 Corinthians 13:13

Love is the first and ultimate requirement for Christian living. Here in 1 Peter that means it has to be practical. In this passage love is embodied in hospitality and service. In this particular context the hospitality may be related initially to welcoming the community into the home where early Christian worship took place. Do so graciously, without complaining. This will have implications for all other ways that we, the church, must be gracious. Hospitality and service go hand in hand.

> List the ways that Christian love is made practical when you exercise hospitality.

Hebrews 13:1-2
¹**Let mutual love continue.** ²**Do not neglect hospitality, for through it some have unknowingly entertained angels.**

If we read Hebrews as a sermon rather than a letter, we are more likely to catch the feel and tone of a persuasive preacher. He wants his hearers to be convinced that Jesus uniquely fulfilled all that Israel had hoped for, even surpassing their expectations. He portrays Jesus as a compassionate High Priest whose own sacrifice is complete and perfect.

The first twelve chapters of Hebrews capture the passion and the purpose of his preaching. The final chapter, Hebrews 13, turns to more mundane, but essential, local concerns. As with Paul and Peter, the author of Hebrews knows that life within the Christian community can become messy and even distracting. Pointed reminders about the essentials of living their faith will serve Jesus' followers well, cementing their bond to Jesus himself.

This passage, like those previously considered, revolves around love and how it is expressed. Hospitality is essential, cannot be ignored or neglected, and is a basic part of being a follower of Christ. But in this passage there is a reward: contact with the divine through God's messengers, angels.

The most graphic example would have surfaced in the minds of those who heard this preacher. Centuries earlier, Abraham and Sarah welcomed three visitors to their campsite at Mamre (Gen 18:1-15), located in the arid southern region of Canaan. As was typical in such a barren, largely nomadic world, the arrival of travelers required some expression of hospitality. Abraham and Sarah, each in their own way, make the guests comfortable by bringing water to bathe and soothe their dirty and tired feet, and by providing a nourishing meal. Abraham spends time in conversation with the travelers and discovers God's plan to bless Sarah with a child. These travelers turned out to be God's messengers, and one of them is even identified as the Lord (18:1). Abraham and Sarah were hospitable to travelers and found they had entertained angels.

How important is listening and conversation to the expression of hospitality?

Every generation of believers may find in this ancestral story and in the promise in Hebrews a motivation for our actions. More deeply, this may heighten our awareness that God inhabits his people. Simple travelers in the desert became God's very presence; simple sojourners in our midst help us to see in them God's presence and the opportunity to serve.

What is your attitude toward those seen as strangers? When has a chance encounter with someone different been an experience of grace for you?

Praying the Word / Sacred Reading

*Pray about what you have been learning and
reflecting upon using your own words or the
words of prayer provided below.*

When Jesus sat at table with his disciples after
washing their feet
he spoke consoling words to them:
"Do not let your hearts be troubled.
You have faith in God; have faith also in me.
In my Father's house there are many dwellings.
If there were not, would I have told you
I am going to prepare a place for you?"
(John 14:1-4)

Give us, Holy Spirit, the same confidence that
Jesus expresses,
that his Father and ours
is the eternal host who provides for his people.
Prod us to become the kind of people who
call upon the grace of God
to welcome others, to make room for others
in our hearts and our daily lives,
and to share liberally as a sign of
our commitment to follow Jesus,
as a sign of God's love for this world.

Disturb us when we are complacent.
Inspire us when we are hesitant.
Forgive us when we are blind to those in our
midst, yet on the fringes.
Warm our hearts with compassion and
creativity.
Give us courage to act.

Living the Word

Here are some possible ways to respond to the message of hospitality in God's Word:

- *Commit to finding out more about those in your neighborhood or parish who look or sound different from you or your family. Do it soon to avoid growing lax or fearful.*

- *Talk with people in your parish or civic community whose organizations address the needs of immigrants or travelers. Find out what the organization actually does, and consider whether you are called to assist in some way.*

- *Resolve to pray regularly that God will provide opportunities to express Christian hospitality to people you meet. Be open to opportunities and be ready to act.*

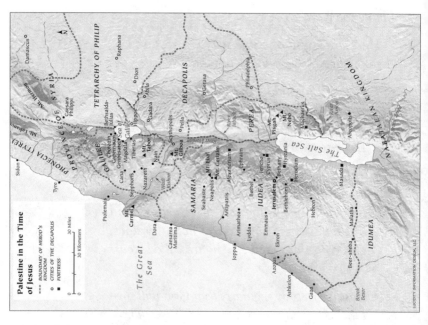

Palestine in the Time
of Jesus

--- BOUNDARY OF HEROD'S
KINGDOM
○ CITIES OF THE DECAPOLIS
■ FORTRESS

0   30 Miles
0   30 Kilometers

PHONECIA (TYRE)
Sidon
Tyre
Mt. Hermon
Damascus
Mt. Lebanon
PROVINCE OF SYRIA
TETRARCHY OF PHILIP
Caesarea
Philippi
Raphana
GALILEE
Dion
Ptolemais
Carmel
Cana
Sepphoris
Nazareth
Chorazin
Capernaum
Bethsaida-
Julias
Sea of Galilee
Magdala
Tiberias
Hippos
Gadara
Abila
DECAPOLIS
Gerasa
Dora
Wadi Mishor
Mt. Tabor
Nain
Gilboa
Scythopolis
Pella
Philadelphia
Caesarea
Maritima
SAMARIA
Seabaste
Neapolis
Mt. Ebal
Mt. Gerizim
Alexandrium
Ephraim
River Jordan
River Jabbok
PEREA
Mt. Nebo
Mt.
Pisgah
Machaerus
Joppa
Antipatris
Arimathea
Lydda
Bethel
Jericho
Cyprus
Bethany
Jerusalem
Herodium
Hyrcania
The Salt Sea
Dead Sea
Callirrhoe
Emmaus
Bethlehem
Ekron
Azotus
Ashkelon
Gaza
Hebron
Beer-sheba
Malatha
Arnon
Masada
ABATAEAN KINGDOM
IDUMEA
Brook Besor
IUDEA
The Great Sea

LUCIDITY INFORMATION DESIGN, LLC

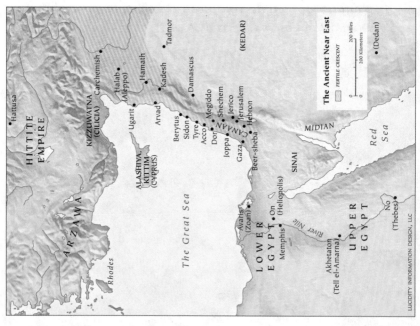

The Ancient Near East

FERTILE CRESCENT

0   200 Miles
0   200 Kilometers

Hattusa
HITTITE
EMPIRE
ARZAWA
KIZZUWATNA
(CILICIA)
Carchemish
Tadmor
Halab
(Aleppo)
Hamath
Kadesh
Damascus
(KEDAR)
(Dedan)
Ugarit
ALASHIYA
KITTIM
(CYPRUS)
Arvad
Berytus
Sidon
Tyre
Acco
Dor
Megiddo
Shechem
Joppa
Jerusalem
Hebron
Gaza
Beer-sheba
CANAAN
Rhodes
The Great Sea
MIDIAN
SINAI
Red Sea
Avaris
(Zoan)
On (Heliopolis)
Memphis
LOWER
EGYPT
River Nile
Akhetaton
(Tell el-Amarna)
UPPER
EGYPT
No
(Thebes)

LUCIDITY INFORMATION DESIGN, LLC